THE FIVE
Purposes
OF MARRIAGE

A VIDEO-BASED STUDY FOR SMALL GROUPS OR COUPLES

By George and Tondra Gregory

THE FIVE PURPOSES OF MARRIAGE
A VIDEO-BASED STUDY FOR SMALL GROUPS OR COUPLES

CSR10785

 **SADDLEBACK CHURCH**

Published by Saddleback Church
1 Saddleback Parkway
Lake Forest, CA 92630

www.saddleback.com

ISBN: 978-1-959074-19-9

CONTENTS

INTRODUCTION *5*

UNDERSTANDING YOUR STUDY GUIDE *6*

How to Use This Video Curriculum *8*

PURPOSE ONE: **HONOR** *11*

PURPOSE TWO: **RELATIONAL INTIMACY** *17*

PURPOSE THREE: **SPIRITUAL INTIMACY** *23*

PURPOSE FOUR: **PARTNERSHIP** *29*

PURPOSE FIVE: **LEGACY** *35*

SMALL GROUP RESOURCES *41*

Helps for Hosts *42*

Frequently Asked Questions *46*

Circles of Life *48*

Small Group Guidelines *49*

Prayer and Praise Report *51*

Small Group Calendar *53*

Key Verses *54*

ANSWER KEY *55*

Small Group Roster *57*

THE FIVE
Purposes
OF MARRIAGE

INTRODUCTION

We're so excited you're taking this opportunity to explore this five-week study on *The Five Purposes of Marriage*. We believe successful marriages need a solid blueprint to follow and build upon. God's Word provides just that and gives us the right vision and tools to build strong marriages.

We wish we had a resource like this when we started off in marriage almost 28 years ago! We desperately needed a better blueprint for marriage than the one we crafted ourselves or what we observed from other couples also struggling to find answers. As leaders of Marriage at Saddleback and Journey for Life, our ministry to married couples, we are passionate about helping marriages uncover the blueprint God designed.

The Five Purposes of Marriage answers the question, "Why did God create marriage?" and sheds light on some of his purposes for bringing you and your spouse together. Each week during this study, we will discuss one of the five purposes for marriage. Here's a brief overview of each purpose:

PURPOSE ONE: HONOR
Honor is placing a high value on your spouse and priority above any other earthly relationship.

PURPOSE TWO: RELATIONAL INTIMACY
Relational intimacy is what helps form an indestructible bond and closeness in your marriage.

PURPOSE THREE: SPIRITUAL INTIMACY
Spiritual intimacy is growing spiritually together in your relationship with God.

PURPOSE FOUR: PARTNERSHIP
Partnership is demonstrating "love in action" towards your spouse.

PURPOSE FIVE: LEGACY
Legacy is reflecting God's image through your marriage to others around you.

May God bless your marriages richly as you invest your time by diving into this study together.

George & Tondra Gregory

George & Tondra Gregory

UNDERSTANDING YOUR STUDY GUIDE

Here is a brief explanation of the features of this study guide.

CHECKING IN

Begin each group conversation by briefly discussing a question or two that will help focus everyone's attention on the subject of the lesson.

KEY VERSE

In each lesson, you will find a key Bible verse for your group to focus on together.

VIDEO LESSON

View the accompanying video for each purpose and follow along with the lesson outline on the pages that follow. There are places you will be prompted to fill in the blanks. Be sure to refer back to outline during your discussion time.

DISCUSSION QUESTIONS

Each video lesson is complemented by several questions for group discussion. Please don't feel pressured to discuss every single question. There is no reason to rush through the answers. Give everyone ample opportunity to share their thoughts. If you don't get through all of the discussion questions, that's okay.

PUTTING IT INTO PRACTICE

This is where the rubber meets the road. We don't just want to be hearers of the Word. We also need to be doers of the Word (James 1:22). These assignments are application exercises that will help you put into practice the truths you have discussed in the lesson.

PRAYER DIRECTION

Spend some time in prayer at the end of each session. Use the brief prompts to help guide your prayer times.

DIVING DEEPER

This section offers suggestions for different ways you can enrich your understanding of that week's lesson.

SMALL GROUP RESOURCES

There are additional small group resources, such as **SMALL GROUP GUIDELINES**, **HELPS FOR HOSTS**, **PRAYER AND PRAISE REPORT**, etc., in the back of this study guide.

How to Use This Video Curriculum

Follow these simple steps for a successful small group meeting:

- Open your group meeting by using the **CHECKING IN** sections of your study.

- Have someone read the **KEY VERSE** aloud and spend a few quiet moments meditating on it.

- Watch the corresponding video together while following the material and filling in the blanks in the **VIDEO LESSON**.

- Spend some time answering the **DISCUSSION QUESTIONS**. Be sure to review the **PUTTING IT INTO PRACTICE** section to help you implement the lessons into your daily life. Commit to fulfilling any assignments before your next lesson.

- Close your time together by following the **PRAYER DIRECTION** suggestions.

- Make sure to look at the **DIVING DEEPER** section for a recommendation on how to continue growing throughout the week.

A Tip for the Host

The study guide material is meant to be your servant, not your master. The point is not to race through the sessions, but to take time to let God work in your lives. It is not necessary to "go around the circle" before you move on to the next question. Give people the freedom to speak, but don't insist on it or make it mandatory. Your group will enjoy deeper, more open sharing and discussion if people don't feel pressured to speak up.

How to Use the Interactive Version of This Study Guide

If you are viewing this study guide in its downloadable form on your tablet, phone, or even your desktop, you will not have to print it out unless you want to. Throughout the guide, you will see areas where you can type directly into the guide. There are also convenient links that direct you to external resources including Scripture passages and suggested interactive activities.

HELPFUL TIP

For the best experience on Android™ platforms, please view this interactive study on Adobe Acrobat Reader DC®.

1 THESSALONIANS 5:11 (NIV)

Therefore encourage one another and build each other up.

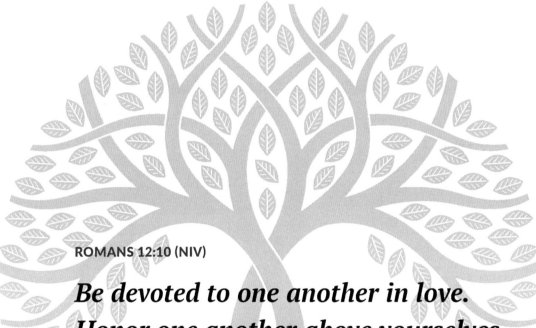

ROMANS 12:10 (NIV)

Be devoted to one another in love.
Honor one another above yourselves.

HONOR

 CHECKING IN

Begin your time together with a few ice-breaker questions about your marriage:

1. How did you two meet?
2. When did you know your spouse was *the one*?
3. Who proposed and how?
4. How long have you been married?

 KEY VERSE

> *Each one of you also must love his wife as he loves himself, and the wife must respect her husband.*

EPHESIANS 5:33 (NIV)

 VIDEO LESSON

Watch the video lesson on Purpose One: Honor. The following pages will have fill in the blanks to complete as you watch the video. Refer back to this outline during your discussion time.

HONOR

- Honor is _____ a high value on your spouse.

  Husbands, love your wives, just as Christ loved the church and gave himself up for her to make her holy, cleansing her by the washing with water through the word , and to present her to himself as a radiant church, without stain or wrinkle or any other blemish, but holy and blameless. In this same way, husbands ought to love their wives as their own bodies. He who loves his wife loves himself.

  However, each one of you also must love his wife as he loves himself, and the wife must respect her husband.

  EPHESIANS 5:25–28, 33 (NIV)

- Honor means _____ for husbands

  than it does for the wives.

- A husband feels honored when he is shown _____ .

- A wife feels honored when she receives _____ .

Developing an Atmosphere of Honor

1. Commit to _____ .

   Be devoted to one another in love. Honor one another above yourselves.

   ROMANS 12:10 (NIV)

   Love is patient, love is kind. It does not envy, it does not boast, it is not proud. It does not dishonor others, it is not self-seeking, it is not easily angered, it keeps no record of wrongs. Love does not delight in evil but rejoices with the truth. It always protects, always trusts, always hopes, always perseveres. Love never fails.

   1 CORINTHIANS 13:4–8 (NIV)

2. _____ each other.

   Therefore encourage one another and build each other up.

   1 THESSALONIANS 5:11 (NIV)

3. _____ each other.

   Do nothing from selfish ambition or conceit, but in humility count others more significant than yourselves. Let each of you look not only to his own interests, but also to the interests of others. Have this mind among yourselves, which is yours in Christ Jesus.

   PHILIPPIANS 2:3–5 (ESV)

4. Express _____ .

   Whatever is true, whatever is honorable, whatever is just, whatever is pure, whatever is lovely, whatever is commendable, if there is any excellence, if there is anything worthy of praise, think about these things. What you have learned and received and heard and seen in me—practice these things, and the God of peace will be with you.

   PHILIPPIANS 4:8–9 (ESV)

5. _____ the need to be right.

   [Love] *does not demand its own way.*

   1 CORINTHIANS 13:5 (NLT)

DISCUSSION QUESTIONS

1. Reread Ephesians 5:25–28, 33 above. What are your impressions of this directive from Paul?

2. George and Tondra talk about how *"honor means something different for husbands than it does for wives."* What makes you feel honored?

3. Building a culture of honor in your marriage requires intentionality. Which elements of an atmosphere of honor (commit to faithfulness, affirm each other, value each other, express gratitude, surrender the need to be right) stood out to you as an area you could commit to working on this week? What are one to two things you will do to grow in that area this week?

PUTTING IT INTO PRACTICE

1. Reflect and respond to the following questions.

    a. **Application:** How can I apply what I learned into my marriage? Where am I willing to grow and sacrifice?

    b. **Revelation:** What did I learn about my spouse? What did I learn about myself?

    c. **Inspiration:** What key insights did you gain from God's Word?

    d. **Appreciation:** How can you show appreciation for your spouse's contribution to each of the purposes?

2. Make it a point to intentionally affirm your spouse or express your gratitude to them this week.

PRAYER DIRECTION

Psalm 139:23–24 says, *Search me, God, and know my heart; test me and know my anxious thoughts.* See if there is any offensive way in me, and lead me in the way everlasting. As a group, pray this prayer over your marriages this week. Ask God to help you recognize anything you're doing that could cause your spouse to feel dishonored. (If needed, ask for forgiveness and repent of that behavior.) Pray for wisdom for how to better honor your spouse.

 DIVING DEEPER

Dive deeper this week by listening to this episode from Saddleback's Doable Discipleship podcast on having honor in your marriage.

LISTEN: *Episode 251—The Five Purposes of Marriage: Honor*

PROVERBS 16:3 (NLT)

Commit your actions to the LORD, and your plans will succeed.

PURPOSE TWO

RELATIONAL INTIMACY

 CHECKING IN

1. Were you able to create an atmosphere of honor in your marriage last week? If so, what were you intentional about doing?

2. How did you notice differences this past week in how husbands and wives feel honored?

 KEY VERSE

> *"For this reason a man will leave his father and mother and be united to his wife, and the two will become one flesh." This is a profound mystery.*

EPHESIANS 5:31–32 (NIV)

 VIDEO LESSON

Watch the video lesson on Purpose Two: Relational Intimacy. The following pages will have fill in the blanks to complete as you watch the video. Refer back to this outline during your discussion time.

RELATIONAL INTIMACY

Relational intimacy is about _____ an indestructible bond and closeness in your marriage.

> *"For this reason a man will leave his father and mother and be united to his wife, and the two will become one flesh." This is a profound mystery.*

EPHESIANS 5:31–32 (NIV)

Developing an Atmosphere of Relational Intimacy

Relational intimacy thrives on trust and safety. Cultivating this requires:

1. _____ and _____: Prioritizing your spouse and not taking each other for granted.

2. _____: Maintaining relational intimacy requires intellectual and emotional connection and bonding.

3. _____ : Time equals love.

   Quality time requires:

   - Being _____ , not _____

   - Making _____

   - Listening to _____

   - Asking _____

   - _____ in your friendship

SEVEN GOALS TO HELP YOU "WIN" IN RESOLVING CONFLICT

Goals	Guiding Scriptures
Goal One: Be gentle.	*A gentle answer turns away wrath, but a harsh word stirs up anger.* **PROVERBS 15:1 (NIV)**
Goal Two: Be willing to concede.	*[Love] does not insist on its own way.* **1 CORINTHIANS 13:5 (ESV)**
Goal Three: Stay calm.	*Whoever restrains his words has knowledge, and he who has a cool spirit is a man of understanding.* **PROVERBS 17:27 (ESV)** *Too much talk leads to sin. Be sensible and keep your mouth shut.* **PROVERBS 10:19 (NLT)**
Goal Four: Be gracious.	*Gracious words are a honeycomb, sweet to the soul and healing to the bones.* **PROVERBS 16:24 (NIV)**
Goal Five: Seek resolution.	*Do not let the sun go down on your anger.* **EPHESIANS 4:26b (ESV)** *See to it that no one falls short of the grace of God and that no bitter root grows up to cause trouble and defile many.* **HEBREWS 12:15 (NIV)**
Goal Six: Speak the truth in love.	*Rather, speaking the truth in love, we are to grow up in every way into him who is the head, into Christ.* **EPHESIANS 4:15 (ESV)**
Goal Seven: Deal with one issue at a time.	*There is a time for everything, and a season for every activity under the heavens.* **ECCLESIASTES 3:1 (NIV)**

 **DISCUSSION QUESTIONS**

1 Why do you think trust and safety are so important for relational intimacy? What happens when it's missing . . . or broken?

2. George and Tondra offered several suggestions for ways to spend time together—things like a daily check in, date nights, doing chores together, evening walks, pillow or coffee talk time. How do you and your spouse make time for each other on a regular basis? If this is a habit you've yet to you're going to start building, what might be a good starting place for you?

3. Our lives are full of distractions that can make relational intimacy really difficult. What are the greatest distractions you face in this season of your life? What might you be able to do to mitigate those distractions?

4. Learning to resolve conflict well is critical to growing and preserving relational intimacy. Review the seven goals that George and Tondra talked about. Which of those goals comes easiest to you? Which is/are more difficult?

PUTTING IT INTO PRACTICE

1. Reflect and respond to the following questions.

   a. **Application:** How can I apply what I learned into my marriage? Where am I willing to grow and sacrifice?

   b. **Revelation:** What did I learn about my spouse? What did I learn about myself?

   c. **Inspiration:** What key insights did you gain from God's Word?

   d. **Appreciation:** How can you show appreciation for your spouse's contribution to each of the purposes?

2. Select one new way you and your spouse can spend time together this week (and then do it).

PRAYER DIRECTION

Proverbs 16:3 (NLT) says, *Commit your actions to the LORD, and your plans will succeed.*

With your spouse, ask God to help in your pursuit of building stronger relational intimacy. Invite him into your conflict resolution and ask him to guide you in growing a secure relationship that values quality time. Thank him for being a part of your relationship—for caring about you both individually and as a couple.

 ## DIVING DEEPER

Dive deeper this week by listening to this episode from Saddleback's Doable Discipleship podcast on having relational intimacy in your marriage.

LISTEN: *Episode 252—The Five Purposes of Marriage: Relational Intimacy*

PSALMS 139:1, 23–24 (NLT)

O LORD, you have examined my heart and know everything about me.

Search me, O God, and know my heart; test me and know my anxious thoughts.

Point out anything in me that offends you, and lead me along the path of everlasting life.

THE FIVE
Purposes
OF MARRIAGE

SPIRITUAL INTIMACY

 CHECKING IN

1. How were you and your spouse able to find some quality time together this last week?

2. Were there any conflicts that brewed up this week? How were you able to apply the seven goals to help you win in conflict resolution?

 KEY VERSE

Bear with each other and forgive one another if any of you has a grievance against someone. Forgive as the Lord forgave you. And over all these virtues put on love, which binds them all together in perfect unity.

COLOSSIANS 3:13–14 (NIV)

 VIDEO LESSON

Watch the video lesson on Purpose Three: Spiritual Intimacy. The following pages will have fill in the blanks to complete as you watch the video. Refer back to this outline during your discussion time.

SPIRITUAL INTIMACY

- Spiritual intimacy means _____ together spiritually

  (individually and as a couple) in our nature and relationship with and in God.

  > *Therefore, as God's chosen people, holy and dearly loved, clothe yourselves with compassion, kindness, humility, gentleness and patience. Bear with each other and forgive one another if any of you has a grievance against someone. Forgive as the Lord forgave you. And over all these virtues put on love, which binds them all together in perfect unity. Let the peace of Christ rule in your hearts, since as members of one body you were called to peace. And be thankful. Let the message of Christ dwell among you richly as you teach and admonish one another with all wisdom through psalms, hymns, and songs from the Spirit, singing to God with gratitude in your hearts. And whatever you do, whether in word or deed, do it all in the name of the Lord Jesus, giving thanks to God the Father through him.*
  >
  > **COLOSSIANS 3:12–17 (NIV)**

- Spiritual intimacy is seeing my _____ to become more

  like Christ lived out and supported by my marriage.

  > *A man shall leave his father and mother and hold fast to his wife, and they shall become one flesh.*
  >
  > **GENESIS 2:24 (ESV)**

- Spiritual intimacy involves seeing my marriage as not something to just make

  me _____ but to make me _____ .

Keys to Building Spiritual Intimacy

1. Realize it takes _____ and _____ .

2. Examine _____ heart.

> O LORD, you have examined my heart
>   and know everything about me .
>
> Search me, O God, and know my heart;
>   test me and know my anxious thoughts.
> Point out anything in me that offends you,
>   and lead me along the path of everlasting life.
>
> **PSALMS 139:1, 23–24 (NLT)**

3. Don't try to force what you do in your devotional time onto your spouse.

4. Be willing to speak into your spouse's life, and let your spouse do the same.

5. Make _____ a priority.

> Don't worry about anything; instead, pray about everything. Tell God
> what you need, and thank him for all he has done. If you do this, you
> will experience God's peace, which is far more wonderful than the
> human mind can understand. His peace will guard your hearts and
> minds as you live in Christ Jesus.
>
> **PHILIPPIANS 4:6–7 (TLB)**

DISCUSSION QUESTIONS

1. It might seem counterintuitive that working on your own relationship with Jesus is a key to spiritual intimacy in your marriage. How have you experienced this in your marriage? If this is a new idea for you, how do you imagine focusing on your own relationship with Jesus could affect your relationship with your spouse?

2. George and Tondra said that it's important to see our marriages not as something to make us happy, but to make us holy. How could having holiness (instead of happiness) as a goal for yourself in your marriage change the way you experience or think about your relationship with your spouse?

3. Speaking truth into your spouse's life (and letting them speak truth into yours) requires a foundation of trust and safety. What might be some barriers (perceived or actual) to this level of communication between you and your spouse? How might they be overcome?

4. Why do you think praying together (not just for each other) is so important for spiritual intimacy?

PUTTING IT INTO PRACTICE

1. Reflect and respond to the following questions.

   a. **Application:** How can I apply what I learned into my marriage? Where am I willing to grow and sacrifice?

   b. **Revelation:** What did I learn about my spouse? What did I learn about myself?

   c. **Inspiration:** What key insights did you gain from God's Word?

   d. **Appreciation:** How can you show appreciation for your spouse's contribution to each of the purposes?

2. As part of your quiet time this week, spend some time reflecting on Psalm 139:1, 23–24 and asking God to help you examine your own heart. Is there something you need to confess to your spouse? Is there something you need to forgive your spouse for?

PRAYER DIRECTION

Break off into couples right now and take time to pray with each other. Thank God for what you are learning and for how he has blessed you. Lift up any prayer requests that have been on your heart.

 ## DIVING DEEPER

Dive deeper this week by listening to this episode from Saddleback's Doable Discipleship podcast on having spiritual intimacy in your marriage.

LISTEN: *Episode 253—The Five Purposes of Marriage: Spiritual Intimacy*

For you have been called to live in freedom . . . [not] freedom to satisfy your sinful nature . . . [but] freedom to serve one another in love.

THE FIVE
Purposes
OF MARRIAGE

PURPOSE FOUR

PARTNERSHIP

🍃 CHECKING IN

1. How was it praying together with your spouse this last week?
2. What is something you are grateful for this week?

🍃 KEY VERSE

*Two people are better off than one, for they can help each
other succeed.*

ECCLESIASTES 4:9 (NLT)

🍃 VIDEO LESSON

Watch the video lesson on Purpose Four: Partnership. The following pages will
have fill in the blanks to complete as you watch the video. Refer back to this
outline during your discussion time.

PARTNERSHIP

Partnership is _____ your "love in action" towards your spouse.

> *Two people are better off than one, for they can help each other succeed. If one person falls, the other can reach out and help. But someone who falls alone is in real trouble. Likewise, two people lying close together can keep each other warm. But how can one be warm alone? A person standing alone can be attacked and defeated, but two can stand back-to-back and conquer.*
>
> **ECCLESIASTES 4:9–12 (NLT)**

Partnership (love in action) involves:

- Joining together two _____ people in a relationship.

- Developing an _____ of each other's differences.

- _____ our differences to serve the needs of one another and others in the church or around us.

CONTRACT VS. COVENANT	
Contract	**Covenant**
Based on legalism and leverage	**Based on love and loyalty**
Lasts as long as both parties agree	**Lasts as long as we live**
Calls for the signing of names	**Calls for the binding of hearts**
Our idea	God's idea

How to Build a Lifelong Partnership

1. Check your own _____ .

    You were taught, with regard to your former way of life, to put off your old self, which is being corrupted by its deceitful desires; to be made new in the attitude of your minds; and to put on the new self, created to be like God in true righteousness and holiness.

    EPHESIANS 4:22–24 (NIV)

2. _____ your spouse's differences.

    I praise you because I am fearfully and wonderfully made; your works are wonderful, I know that full well.

    PSALM 139:14 (NIV)

3. _____ on each other's strengths and _____

    each other's weaknesses.

    Two people are better off than one, for they can help each other succeed. If one person falls, the other can reach out and help. But someone who falls alone is in real trouble. Likewise, two people lying close together can keep each other warm. But how can one be warm alone? A person standing alone can be attacked and defeated, but two can stand back-to-back and conquer.

    ECCLESIASTES 4:9–12 (NLT)

4. _____ and _____ the needs of your spouse.

    For you have been called to live in freedom . . . [not] freedom to satisfy your sinful nature . . . [but] <u>freedom to serve one another in love</u>.

    GALATIANS 5:13 (NLT)

5. _____ your needs to one another.

DISCUSSION QUESTIONS

1. Why is it so important that marriage be approached as a covenant, rather than a contract? What are the risks of approaching marriage as a contract?

2. George and Tondra encouraged us to appreciate each other's differences. What is one way your spouse is different than you that you have learned (or are learning) to appreciate?

3. The ability to share your needs with your spouse is essential to a healthy marriage. Is it easy or difficult for you to share your needs with your spouse? Why?

4. Active listening means listening for understanding (without becoming defensive). When your spouse shares one of their needs with you, how does that make you feel?

PUTTING IT INTO PRACTICE

1. Reflect and respond to the following questions.

   a. **Application:** How can I apply what I learned into my marriage? Where am I willing to grow and sacrifice?

   b. **Revelation:** What did I learn about my spouse? What did I learn about myself?

   c. **Inspiration:** What key insights did you gain from God's Word?

   d. **Appreciation:** How can you show appreciation for your spouse's contribution to each of the purposes?

PRAYER DIRECTION

On your own, make a list of the way your spouse is unique/different from you. Then spend some time thanking God for the way He made your spouse and pray for the eyes to see and appreciate how those differences are actually God's provision to complement your own weaknesses.

 DIVING DEEPER

Dive deeper this week by listening to this episode from Saddleback's Doable Discipleship podcast on having partnership in your marriage.

LISTEN: *Episode 254—The Five Purposes of Marriage: Partnership*

GALATIANS 5:22–23 (NIV)

But the fruit of the Spirit is love, joy, peace, patience, kindness, goodness, faithfulness, gentleness and self-control.

PURPOSE FIVE

LEGACY

🍃 CHECKING IN

1. How have you viewed partnership with your spouse differently this past week?

2. What has been your biggest takeaway from this study?

🍃 KEY VERSE

So God created man in His own image. . . . Then God blessed them, and God said to them, "Be fruitful and multiply; fill the earth."

GENESIS 1:27–28 (NKJV)

🍃 VIDEO LESSON

Watch the video lesson on Purpose Five: Legacy. The following pages will have fill in the blanks to complete as you watch the video. Refer back to this outline during your discussion time.

LEGACY

- Legacy is _____ God's image through your marriage to others around you.

   So God created man in His own image. ... Then God blessed them, and God said to them, "Be fruitful and multiply; fill the earth.

   GENESIS 1:27–28 (NKJV)

- Marriage should carry the message of the gospel which communicates

   _____ and _____ to others.

   Many of the Samaritans from that town believed in him because of the woman's testimony, "He told me everything I ever did." So when the Samaritans came to him, they urged him to stay with them, and he stayed two days. And because of his words many more became believers.

   JOHN 4:39–41 (NIV)

- What _____ will our marriage tell or leave behind?

- Our marriage and relationships are a _____

   _____ .

   Then God said, "Let us make mankind in our image, in our likeness ..."

   GENESIS 1:26 (NIV)

   But the fruit of the Spirit is love, joy, peace, patience, kindness, goodness, faithfulness, gentleness and self-control.

   GALATIANS 5:22–23 (NIV)

   Be kind and compassionate to one another, forgiving each other, just as in Christ God forgave you.

   EPHESIANS 4:32 (NIV)

How to Build a Marriage that Intentionally Mirrors God's Image

1. _____ your past and release your spouse from his/hers.

2. _____ to living an integrated life.

3. _____ often and effectively.

CONCLUDING PRAYER

With this study coming to a close, set aside some time to pray for the marriages represented in your group. You may use this prayer as a guide to pray together as a whole group or have couples spend this time praying with each other.

Father, we pray as we close out our study on The Five Purposes of Marriage, *would you help each couple to commit and live a life of:*

- *Honoring one another*
- *Building an indestructible bond through their Relational Intimacy*
- *Growing together in Spiritual Intimacy with each other and you*
- *Demonstrating love in action through their Partnership*
- *Empowering them to reflect your image through their Legacy*

In Jesus' name we pray,
Amen.

 ## DISCUSSION QUESTIONS

1. In what ways could the story of your marriage communicate hope and redemption to others?

2. Our marriages are meant to tell the world something about the story of the gospel. How does hearing that make you feel? What does it make you think about?

3. Thinking back over the five purposes of marriage (**Honor, Relational Intimacy, Spiritual Intimacy, Partnership,** and **Legacy**), what are the areas of strength in your marriage today? In what areas do you see the opportunity to grow/invest?

PUTTING IT INTO PRACTICE

1. Reflect and respond to the following questions.

   a. **Application:** How can I apply what I learned into my marriage? Where am I willing to grow and sacrifice?

   b. **Revelation:** What did I learn about my spouse? What did I learn about myself?

   c. **Inspiration:** What key insights did you gain from God's Word?

   d. **Appreciation:** How can you show appreciation for your spouse's contribution to each of the purposes?

2. What is the story of your marriage so far? Where or how have you seen God show up for you? Take time to write it out together.

PRAYER DIRECTION

A healthy marriage balances all of the five purposes of marriage. As a group, pray that the lessons learned from this study will continue to impact and grow your marriages. Thank God for the gift of marriage and for the legacy that your marriage can and will have.

 ## DIVING DEEPER

Dive deeper this week by listening to this episode from Saddleback's Doable Discipleship podcast on leaving a legacy in your marriage.

LISTEN: *Episode 255—The Five Purposes of Marriage: Legacy*

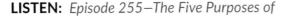

THE FIVE
Purposes
OF MARRIAGE

SMALL GROUP RESOURCES

HELPS FOR HOSTS *42*

FREQUENTLY ASKED QUESTIONS *46*

CIRCLES OF LIFE *48*

SMALL GROUP GUIDELINES *49*

PRAYER AND PRAISE REPORT *51*

SMALL GROUP CALENDAR *53*

KEY VERSES *54*

SMALL GROUP ROSTER *57*

HELPS FOR HOSTS

Congratulations! As the host of your small group, you have responded to the call to help shepherd Jesus' flock. Few other tasks in the family of God surpass the contribution you will be making. As you prepare to facilitate your group, whether it is for one session or for the entire series, here are a few thoughts to keep in mind.

Remember, you are not alone. God knows everything about you, and he knew you would be asked to facilitate your group. You may not feel ready; this is a common feeling all good hosts have! God promises, *"I will never leave you; I will never abandon you"* (Hebrews 13:5 NCV). Whether you are facilitating for one evening, several weeks, or a lifetime, you will be blessed as you serve.

1. **Don't try to do it alone. Pray right now for God to help you build a healthy team.** If you can enlist a co-host to help you shepherd the group, you will find your experience much richer. This is your chance to involve as many people as you can in building a healthy group. All you have to do is to ask people to help. You'll be surprised at the response.

2. **Be friendly and be yourself. God wants to use your unique gifts and temperament.** Be sure to greet people at the door with a big smile—this can set the mood for the whole gathering. Remember, they are taking as big of a step by showing up for this study as you are hosting a small group! Don't try to do things exactly like another host; do them in a way that fits you. Admit when you don't have an answer and apologize when you make a mistake. Your group will love you for it, and you'll sleep better at night.

3. **Prepare for your meeting ahead of time.** Review the session and write down your responses to each question. Pay special attention to the Putting It into Practice section that focuses on applying what you have learned in each lesson. This section will also help your group live what the Bible teaches, not just talk about it.

4. **Pray for your group members by name. Before your group arrives, take a few moments an**d pray for each member by name. Ask God to use your time together to touch the heart of each person in your group. Expect God to lead you to whomever he wants you to encourage or challenge in a special way. If you listen, God will surely lead.

5. **When you ask a question, be patient. Someone will eventually respond.** Sometimes people need a moment or two of silence to think about the question. If silence doesn't bother you, it won't bother anyone else. After someone responds, affirm the response with a simple, "Thanks," or, "Great answer." Then ask, "How about somebody else?" or, "Would someone who hasn't shared like to add anything?" Be sensitive to new people or reluctant members who aren't ready to say, pray, or do anything. If you give them a safe setting, they will blossom over time. If someone in your group is a wallflower who sits silently through every session, consider talking to that person privately and encouraging them to participate. Let them know how important they are to you—that they are loved and appreciated, and that the group would value their input. Remember, still water often runs deep.

6. **Provide transitions between questions.** Ask if anyone would like to read the paragraph or Bible passage. Don't call on anyone, but ask for a volunteer, and then be patient until someone begins. Be sure to thank the person who reads aloud.

7. **Break into smaller groups occasionally.** With a greater opportunity to talk in a small circle, people will connect more with the study, apply more quickly what they're learning, and ultimately get more out of their small group experience. A small circle also encourages a quiet person to participate and tends to minimize the effects of a more vocal or dominant member.

8. **Small circles are also helpful during prayer time.** People who are unaccustomed to praying aloud will feel more comfortable trying it with just two or three others. Also, prayer requests won't take as much time, so circles will have more time to actually pray. When you gather back with the whole group, you can have one person from each circle briefly update everyone on the prayer requests from their subgroups. The other great aspect of subgrouping is that it fosters leadership development. As you ask people in the group to facilitate discussion or to lead a prayer circle, it gives them a small leadership step that can build their confidence.

9. **Rotate facilitators occasionally.** You may be perfectly capable of hosting each time, but you will help others grow in their faith and gifts if you give them opportunities to host the group.

10. **One final challenge (for new or first-time hosts).** Before your first opportunity to lead, look up each of the six passages listed below. Read each one as a devotional exercise to help prepare you with a shepherd's heart. Trust us on this one. If you do this, you will be more than ready for your first meeting.

When he saw the crowds, he had compassion on them, because they were harassed and helpless, like sheep without a shepherd. Then he said to his disciples, "The harvest is plentiful but the workers are few. Ask the Lord of the harvest, therefore to send out workers into his harvest field."

MATTHEW 9:36-38

"I am the good shepherd; I know my sheep and my sheep know me—just as the Father knows me and I know the Father—and I lay down my life for the sheep."

JOHN 10:14-15

Be shepherds of God's flock that is under your care, watching over them—not because you must, but because you are willing, as God wants you to be; not pursuing dishonest gain, but eager to serve; not lording it over those entrusted to you, but being examples to the flock. And when the Chief Shepherd appears, you will receive the crown of glory that will never fade away.

1 PETER 5:2-4

Therefore, if you have any encouragement from being united with Christ, if any comfort from his love, if any common sharing in the Spirit, if any tenderness and compassion, then make my joy complete by being like-minded, having the same love, being one in spirit and of one mind. Do nothing out of selfish ambition or vain conceit. Rather, in humility value others above yourselves, not looking to your own interests but each of you to the interests of the others.

In your relationships with one another, have the same mindset as Christ Jesus.

PHILIPPIANS 2:1-5

Let us hold unswervingly to the hope we profess, for he who promised is faithful. And let us consider how we may spur one another on toward love and good deeds, not giving up meeting together, as some are in the habit of doing, but encouraging one another—and all the more as you see the Day approaching.

HEBREWS 10:23–25 (NIV)

But we were gentle among you, like a mother caring for her little children. We loved you so much that we were delighted to share with you not only the gospel of God but our lives as well, because you had become so dear to us . . . For you know that we dealt with each of you as a father deals with his own children, encouraging, comforting and urging you to live lives worthy of God, who calls you into his kingdom and glory.

1 THESSALONIANS 2:7–8, 11–12 (NIV)

FREQUENTLY ASKED QUESTIONS

HOW LONG WILL THIS GROUP MEET?

This study is five sessions long. We encourage your group to add an extra session for a celebration. In your final session, each group member may decide if he or she desires to continue on for another study. At that time, you may also want to do some informal evaluation, discuss your group guidelines, and decide which study you want to do next. We recommend you visit *saddleback.com/watch* for more video-based small group studies.

WHO IS THE HOST?

The host is the person who coordinates and facilitates your group meetings. In addition to a host, we encourage you to select one or more group members to lead your group discussions. Several other responsibilities can be rotated, including refreshments, prayer requests, worship, or keeping up with those who miss a meeting. Shared ownership in the group helps everyone grow.

WHERE DO WE FIND NEW GROUP MEMBERS?

Recruiting new members can be a challenge for groups, especially new groups with just a few people, or existing groups that lose a few people along the way. We encourage you to use the **CIRCLES OF LIFE** diagram on page **48** of this study guide to brainstorm a list of people from your workplace, church, school, neighborhood, family, and so on. Then pray for the people on each member's list. Allow each member to invite several people from their list. Some groups fear that newcomers will interrupt the intimacy that members have built over time. However, groups that welcome newcomers generally gain strength with the infusion of "new blood." Remember, the next person you add just might become a friend for eternity. Logistically, groups find different ways to add members. Some groups remain permanently open, while others choose to open periodically, such as at the beginning or end of a study. If your group becomes too large for easy, face-to-face conversations, you can subgroup, forming a second discussion group in another room.

HOW DO WE HANDLE THE CHILDCARE NEEDS IN OUR GROUP?

Childcare needs must be handled very carefully. This is a sensitive issue. We suggest you seek creative solutions as a group. One common solution is to have the adults meet in the living room and share the cost of a babysitter (or two) who can be with the kids in another part of the house. Another popular option is to have one supervised home for the kids and a second home (close by) for the adults. If desired, the adults could rotate the responsibility of providing a lesson for the kids. This last option is great with school-age kids and can be a huge blessing to families.

CIRCLES OF LIFE

DISCOVER WHO YOU CAN CONNECT IN COMMUNITY

Use this chart to help carry out one of the values in the **SMALL GROUP GUIDELINES**, to "Welcome Newcomers."

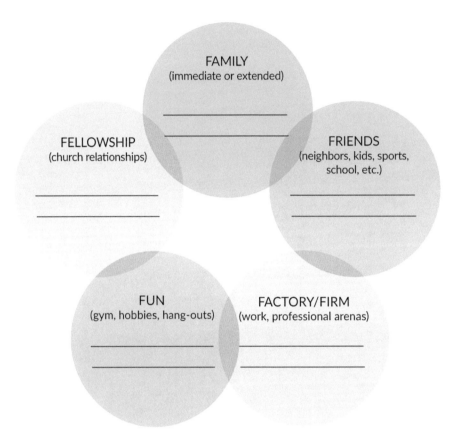

Follow this simple three-step process:

1. List one to two people in each circle.

2. Prayerfully select one person or couple from your list and tell your group about them.

3. Give them a call and invite them to your next meeting. Over fifty percent of those invited to a small group say, "Yes!"

SMALL GROUP GUIDELINES

It's a good idea for every group to put words to their shared values, expectations, and commitments. Such guidelines will help you avoid unspoken agendas and unmet expectations. We recommend you discuss your guidelines during your meeting in order to lay the foundation for a healthy group experience. Feel free to modify anything that does not work for your group.

We agree to the following values:

CLEAR PURPOSE

To grow healthy spiritual lives by building a healthy small group community

GROUP ATTENDANCE

To give priority to the group meeting (call if I am absent or late)

SAFE ENVIRONMENT

To create a safe place where people can be heard and feel loved (no quick answers, snap judgments, or simple fixes)

BE CONFIDENTIAL

To keep anything that is shared strictly confidential and within the group

CONFLICT RESOLUTION

To avoid gossip and to immediately resolve any concerns by following the principles of Matthew 18:15–17

SPIRITUAL HEALTH

To give group members permission to speak into my life and help me live a healthy, balanced spiritual life that is pleasing to God

LIMIT OUR FREEDOM

To limit our freedom by not serving or consuming alcohol during small group meetings or events so as to avoid causing a weaker brother or sister to stumble (1 Corinthians 8:1–13; Romans 14:19–21)

WELCOME NEWCOMERS

To invite friends who might benefit from this study and warmly welcome newcomers

BUILD RELATIONSHIPS

To get to know the other members of the group and pray for them regularly

Other _____

We have also discussed and agree on the following items:

CHILDCARE _____

STARTING TIME _____

ENDING TIME _____

If you haven't already done so, take a few minutes to fill out the **SMALL GROUP CALENDAR** on page **52**.

PRAYER AND PRAISE REPORT

This is a place where you can write each other's requests for prayer. You can also make a note when God answers a prayer. Pray for each other's requests. If you're new to group prayer, it's okay to pray silently or to pray by using just one sentence:

"God, please help _____ to _____."

DATE	PERSON	PRAYER REQUEST	PRAISE REPORT

SMALL GROUP CALENDAR

Healthy groups share responsibilities and group ownership. It might take some time for this to develop. Shared ownership ensures that responsibility for the group doesn't fall to one person. Use the calendar to keep track of social events, mission projects, birthdays, or days off. Complete this calendar at your first or second meeting. Planning ahead will increase attendance and shared ownership.

DATE	LESSON	LOCATION	FACILITATOR	SNACK OR MEAL
	PURPOSE 1			
	PURPOSE 2			
	PURPOSE 3			
	PURPOSE 4			
	PURPOSE 5			

ADDITIONAL RESOURCES

MARRIAGE AT SADDLEBACK CHURCH

Saddleback Church Marriage Ministry

Give your marriage the tools and community needed to thrive through Saddleback's Marriage Ministry. At *saddleback.com/marriage* you'll find information on Couples Night Out, a large-group gathering for married couples. You can also learn how to join or start a couples small group and how to receive couples counseling. Take the next step you need to bring your marriage into a new season of growth.

THIS IS OUR STORY: GENESIS

Saddleback Church Small Group Study

The stories we tell shape who we are. The problem is, the stories we often tell ourselves are tired, bent, and broken. They may come from a painful past, some past wounds, or falsehoods we've chosen to hold onto. These stories shape how we view ourselves, how the world works, even who God is. The Bible, God's story, begins by telling you that you are deeply loved by the Creator of the universe, that you live in a world desperate for good, and that you have a purpose far beyond chasing happiness or just waiting for heaven. This five-session study will lead your small group through the first four chapters of Genesis. Explore what these ancient, God-inspired, life-changing chapters teach us about who God is, what this world is really like, and who we are as humans. Available at *amazon.com*.

THE PURPOSE, PRACTICE, AND POWER OF PRAYER: STRATEGIES FOR SPIRITUAL WARFARE

Saddleback Church Small Group Study

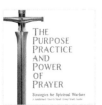

The Scripture makes it clear that we are in a great cosmic battle. It is not a battle against people. It is a battle against spiritual forces of evil that are trying to destroy the work of God—in the world, and in our lives. But God has equipped us, empowered us, authorized us, and called us to partner with him in accomplishing his purposes on the earth. And we do it primarily through prayer. This six-session, video-based study for small groups or individuals will help equip you to pray with greater purpose and power. Available at *amazon.com*.

KEY VERSES

PURPOSE ONE

Each one of you also must love his wife as he loves himself, and the wife must respect her husband.

EPHESIANS 5:33 (NIV)

PURPOSE TWO

"For this reason a man will leave his father and mother and be united to his wife, and the two will become one flesh." This is a profound mystery.

EPHESIANS 5:31–32 (NIV)

PURPOSE THREE

Bear with each other and forgive one another if any of you has a grievance against someone. Forgive as the Lord forgave you. And over all these virtues put on love, which binds them all together in perfect unity.

COLOSSIANS 3:13–14 (NIV)

PURPOSE FOUR

Two people are better off than one, for they can help each other succeed.

ECCLESIASTES 4:9 (NLT)

PURPOSE FIVE

So God created man in His own image. ... Then God blessed them, and God said to them, "Be fruitful and multiply; fill the earth."

GENESIS 1:27–28 (NKJV)

ANSWER KEY

PURPOSE ONE

HONOR

- Honor is **PLACING** a high value on your spouse.
- Honor means **SOMETHING DIFFERENT** for husbands than it does for the wives.
- A husband feels honored when he is shown **RESPECT**.
- A wife feels honored when she receives **SECURE LOVE**.

Developing an Atmosphere of Honor

1. Commit to **FAITHFULNESS**.
2. **AFFIRM** each other.
3. **VALUE** each other.
4. Express **GRATITUDE**.
5. **SURRENDER** the need to be right.

PURPOSE TWO

RELATIONAL INTIMACY

Relational intimacy is about **BUILDING** and indestructible bond and closeness in your marriage.

Developing an Atmosphere of Relational Intimacy

1. **INTENTIONALITY** and **PLANNING**: Prioritizing your spouse and not taking each other for granted.
2. **EMOTIONAL CONNECTION**: Maintaining relational intimacy requires intellectual and emotional connection and bonding.
3. **TIME**: Time equals love.

Quality time requires:

- Being **FOCUSED**, not **DISTRACTED**
- Making **EYE CONTACT**
- Listening to **UNDERSTAND**
- Asking **DEEP QUESTIONS**
- **INVESTING** in your friendship

PURPOSE THREE

SPIRITUAL INTIMACY

- Spiritual Intimacy means **GROWING** together spiritually (individually and as a couple) in our nature and relationship with and in God.
- Spiritual intimacy is seeing my **COMMITMENT** to become more like Christ lived out and supported by my marriage.
- Spiritual intimacy involves seeing my marriage as not something to just make me **HAPPY** but to make me **HOLY**.

Keys to Building Spiritual Intimacy

1. Realize it takes **TIME** and **INTENTIONALITY**.
2. Examine **YOUR OWN** heart.
5. Make **PRAYER** a priority.

PURPOSE FOUR

PARTNERSHIP

Partnership is **SHOWING** your "love in action" towards your spouse.

- Joining together two **DIFFERENT** people in a relationship.
- Developing an **APPRECIATION** of each other's differences.
- **NEGOTIATING** our differences to serve the needs of one another and others in the church or around us.

How to Build a Lifelong Partnership

1. Check your own **ATTITUDE**.
2. **APPRECIATE** your spouse's differences.
3. **BUILD** on each other's strengths and **COMPLEMENT** each other's weaknesses.
4. **UNDERSTAND** and **MEET** the needs of your spouse.
5. **COMMUNICATE** your needs to one another.

LEGACY

- Legacy is **REFLECTING** God's image through your marriage to others around you.

- Marriage should carry the message of the gospel which communicates **HOPE** and **REDEMPTION** to others.

- What **STORY** will our marriage tell or leave behind?

- Our marriage and relationships are a **REFLECTION OF GOD'S IMAGE**.

How to Build a Marriage that Intentionally Mirrors God's Image

1. **CONFESS** your past and release your spouse from his/hers.

2. **COMMIT** to living an integrated life.

3. **COMMUNICATE** often and effectively.

SMALL GROUP ROSTER

NAME	PHONE	EMAIL
1.		
2.		
3.		
4.		
5.		
6.		
7.		
8.		
9.		
10.		
11.		
12.		
13.		
14.		
15.		
16.		

Made in the USA
Las Vegas, NV
11 April 2023